MW01622676
The Mountain
Pond
Little Kicker
Country
where we live
Tony the Pony's
clover patch
Emma Cow's mountain path
Farmer John's barn
Watercress Patch
Sandy the Sow
Pig's mud hole
Daddy & Mother
Donkey's grazing
spot
Little Kicker's
kicking circle

To Luke

♡

Sandy Sprott

2018

Little Kicker
Wants a Turn

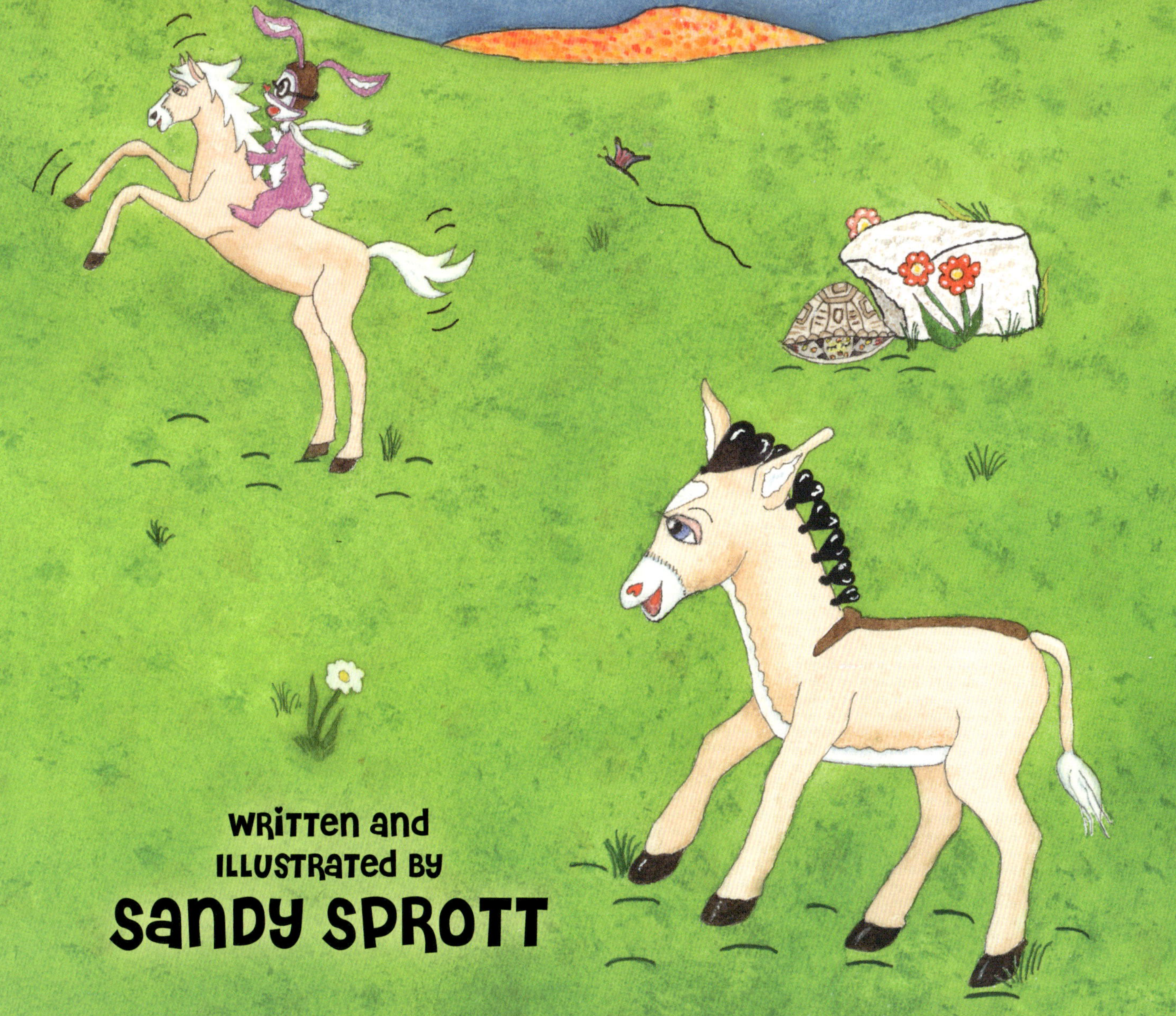

Written and
Illustrated by
Sandy Sprott

Little Kicker
wants a turn

This

Little Kicker book

is presented to

NAME

by

NAME OF RELATIVE, FRIEND, CHURCH OR ORGANIZATION

OCCASION DATE

Little Kicker Wants a Turn

Published by Kimble Creek Press LLC, Hermitage, Missouri
Cover and text design by Amy Cole, jpldesignsolutions.com
Editing by Sam Sprott

Publisher's Cataloging-in-Publication data
Sprott, Sandy.
Little Kicker Wants a Turn / Sandy Sprott.
p. cm.
ISBN 978-0-9843956-6-8 (Hardcover)
ISBN 978-0-9843956-7-5 (pbk.)
Summary : Little Kicker faces rejection when he is not chosen to play with his friends,
but Mother Donkey teaches Little Kicker that God has a plan.
[1. Donkeys --Fiction. 2. Prayer --Fiction. 3. Friendship --Fiction.
4. Animal babies --Fiction. 5. Christian fiction.] I. Title.
PZ7.S7688 Li 2014
[E]-dc22 2014900766

Manufactured by Color House Graphics, Inc., Grand Rapids, MI, USA
March 2014
Job #41971
www.LittleKicker.com

MADE IN U.S.A.

This book is dedicated to our sweet daughter-in-law, Tammy. You joined our family when I was painting our first book. Your creative thinking suggested 'Tammy the Turtle' might be added. I edited the story a bit, learned to draw a turtle, and you became a delightful member of the Little Kicker cast. Sam and I love you beyond the rim of time, and we are blessed by your enduring faith in Jesus.

Rachael the Little Red Hen finished a delicious breakfast of corn. She was eager to play with Becky the Bunny. Becky amused the other animals in Little Kicker Country by wearing different kinds of hats. Some were funny looking…especially since they had to fit around large bunny ears.

"What will she be today?" wondered Rachael as she ran toward Becky's bunny hole home.

Out hopped Becky the Bunny. She was wearing a pilot's flying-ace cap on her head, goggles on her eyes and a white silk scarf around her neck.

"Come on, Rach," said Becky the Bunny as she handed Rachael a pair of goggles and a white silk scarf. "We are going to be pilots and fly airplanes today."

Becky the Bunny did look funny. Her large ears were flapping and flopping around the tight fitting cap. With each bunny hop, one large ear would flap up while the other ear would flop down.

Rachael the Little Red Hen was wondering what they would use for airplanes.

They ran to see Tony the Pony, Emma Cow, Sam the Lamb and Sandy the Sow Pig. Little Kicker and Mother Donkey joined the animals. Daddy Donkey was at work in the fields with Farmer John. Tammy the Turtle was fast asleep.

"We want you to be our airplanes and race across the field with us on your backs," said Becky the Bunny. "We will all have a turn to play."

"Cluck, cluck," said Rachael the Little Red Hen. "Will you play with us?"

The animals smiled at Becky the Bunny and Rachael the Little Red Hen. Those two are always fun to play with!

Becky the Bunny climbed onto the back of Sandy the Sow Pig. Off they ran. Sandy the Sow Pig squealed, "Oink, oink," as she ran with Becky bouncing on her back.

Rachael the Little Red Hen flew onto the back of Sam the Lamb and held tightly to his soft, fluffy wool. She felt safe there. "Baa, baa," bleated Sam the Lamb as they raced down the meadow.

Emma Cow and Mother Donkey decided that they did not want to run.

After a while, Becky the Bunny and Sandy the Sow Pig ran back to the other animals.

Becky wanted to give Tony the Pony a turn to be an airplane and carry her on his back.

Becky the Bunny hoped that Rachael would bring Sam the Lamb back and choose Little Kicker to be her airplane. Becky wanted Little Kicker to have a turn to play.

Rachael the Little Red Hen felt safe holding on to Sam the Lamb's soft wool. She did not want Little Kicker to be her next airplane. Rachael was afraid she would fall off Little Kicker's smooth back.

"Whinny," called Tony the Pony as he stood on his two back legs. Becky the Bunny had to hold on very tightly. Tony tried to catch up with the little hen riding on the back of Sam the Lamb.

Sandy the Sow Pig was
thankful for a rest.

Once again they raced down the field. Tony the Pony and Sam the Lamb shouted and laughed. They liked to play pilots and airplanes. They pretended they were flying down the ridges of the field and over the banks of the stream.

Becky the Bunny, Tony the Pony, Rachael the Little Red Hen and Sam the Lamb were having a lot of giggly fun.

Little Kicker was watching his friends. Now, he wanted a turn to play. His friends were having fun. They had forgotten that Little Kicker had not had his turn to play.

Little Kicker felt sad and lonely. A big, donkey tear came into his eye. He wanted to play, too. For some reason he had never carried anything on his back. He wanted to pretend he was an airplane and run across the field with a pilot on his back.

"Hee Haw," sobbed Little Kicker. "Why am I never chosen to carry anything on my back?" Tears ran down his cheek.

"Now, now," Hee hawed Mother Donkey. She nudged Little Kicker gently and wrapped her tail around him.

"Your time will come, dear. Your strong back and sure feet will carry something or someone very important some day. Just wait, you will see… God has a special plan for you."

"Mom," said Little Kicker, "It is hard to wait. Will you pray for me? Pray that I can use my strong back to carry something or someone very important when I grow up a little more."

“Yes, dear,” said Mother Donkey. “I will pray for you.”

“Dear Lord, please be with Little Kicker. Please let him do something special for You someday. Please let him use his strong back to carry something or someone very important. Little Kicker will try very hard to do a good job. We love you, Lord, Amen.”

"Thank you, Mother," said Little Kicker, "I am happy now. I always feel better when you pray for me."

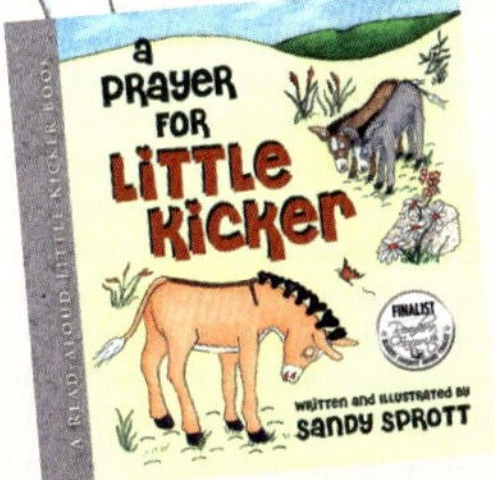

A Prayer For Little Kicker (Little Kicker is prayed for by family and friends.)

Little Kicker's First Rainstorm (Little Kicker is taught to pray to overcome his fears.)

Little Kicker Visits Doctor Quickwell (Little Kicker prays, and God sends an answer.)

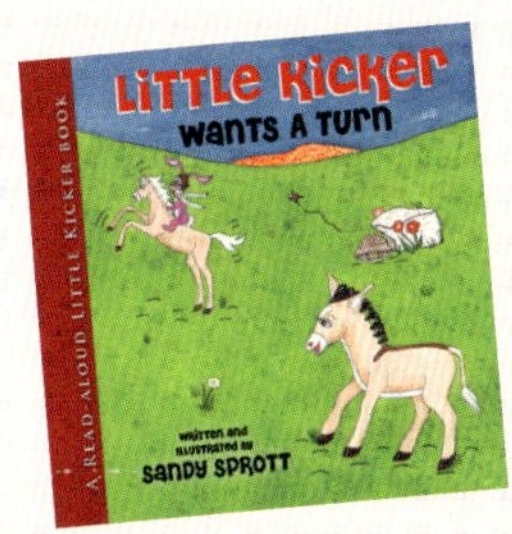

Little Kicker Wants A Turn (Little Kicker faces rejection when he is not chosen to play with his friends, but Mother Donkey teaches Little Kicker that God has a plan.)

coming soon!

Little Kicker Likes To Jump (Little Kicker plans his gigantic jump over Kimble Creek's watercress patch, causing Becky the Bunny to worry about her favorite snack.)

www.littlekicker.com

www.facebook.com/littlekickerbooks

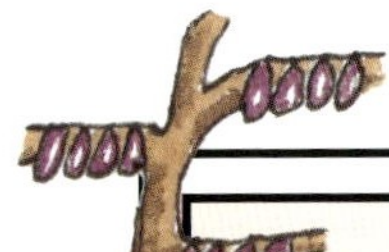

Fun Activities for Children

1. Finding the differences: How are the same animals different on page 7 than they are on page 9?

2. How many colors are in the tree on page 11? Can you name the colors?

3. On page 12, which bunny ear is up? Which bunny ear is down?

4. What is Tammy the Turtle doing on page 13?

5. How many animals are on pages 14 & 15? Do you remember their names? (See pages 12 & 13)

6. What is Tony the Pony doing on page 22?

7. What is running down Little Kicker's cheek on page 27? How many teardrops are there?

8. What made Little Kicker happy? (See Page 30.)

As parents and guardians, it may be hard to watch your child struggle when being forgotten or left out of games. We can't always control how others will treat our children. However, we can reinforce the knowledge in our children that they are treasures in the eyes of Christ, and that He is their constant companion and friend. When we encourage our children to turn to the Lord in times of loneliness or rejection, we are building an unshakable foundation that supports their spiritual life and their trust in the Lord.